INDIAN RECIPES

*

CURRIES

The Publisher would like to thank
Hotel Holiday Inn Crown Plaza, New Delhi and
Maurya Sheraton Hotel and Towers, New Delhi
for the preparation of the dishes, and for giving
permission to photograph them.

ISBN: 1-85605-297-4

Published by **Blitz Editions**
an imprint of
Bookmart Limited
Registered Number 2372865
Trading as Bookmart Limited
Desford Road
Enderby, Leicester, LE9 5AD

Project Coordinator: Padmini Mehta
Photographs: Neeraj Paul & Dheeraj Paul
Design: Sarita Verma Mathur
Typesetting: Monika Gupta

Printed and bound by
Star Standard Industries Pte. Ltd., Singapore

INDIAN RECIPES
*
CURRIES

Blitz Editions

INTRODUCTION
※

A common belief is that all Indian food is 'curry'. Curry is the gravy—a combination of herbs and spices cooked to make a flavoured, aromatic base for a variety of fish, poultry, mutton and vegetables. All curries do not taste alike. The extensive range of spices available can give a feast of flavours, diverse and unusual. The spices and herbs enhance and enliven the taste of the food cooked.

Another misconception is that Indian curries are hot, spicy and rich. The fact is that the food will be spicy and rich as one chooses to make it depending on the amount of chillies used. The rich ingredients can be toned down without affecting the flavour, aroma or the texture of the curry.

The Indian subcontinent is the home of curries. The ancients discovered the preservative properties of spices and used them to cook their food to keep it fresh and edible for longer periods in the hot and humid climates of the region. Every spice is a preservative, antiseptic and digestive. Spices are rich in vitamins as well as in their medicinal value.

There are hundreds of curries—meat, fish, lobsters, poultry or vegetables— depending on the region. Each region has its own flavour and aroma, each more tantalising than the other, tempting you to turn from a gourmand to a gourmet.

CURRIES

— ❋ —

Chicken

Pot Cooked Chicken	6
Butter Chicken	8
Saag Chicken	10
Afghani Chicken	11
Chicken Shahjahani	12
Chicken Stuffed with Nuts	14
Murgh Begam-Bahar	16
Kesari Chicken	17
Chicken Navrattan Korma	18
Fried Chicken Curry	20
Murgh-e-Khas	22
Tangy Chicken	23

Fish

Prawn Curry	24
Goan Fish Curry	26
Fish in Yoghurt	27
Baked Prawns with Pomegranate	28
Mahi Musallam	30
Fish Curry	32

Lamb

Pickled Lamb Chops	34
Lamb with whole Spice	36
Kohe Awadh	38
Nahari Gosht	40
Lamb Rogan Josh	42
Kareli ka Rogan Josh	44
Lamb Nilgiri Korma Curry	45
Lamb Do Piaza	46

Vegetarian

Mattar Makhana Korma	48
Zafrani Kofta Curry	50
Cashewnut Mushroom Curry	51
Curried Aubergine	52
Daal Makhani	54
Palak Paneer	56
Shahi Paneer	57
Kadhi	58
Potato Creole	60
Buttered Vegetables	61

POT COOKED CHICKEN

SERVES: 4

Also called** Murgh Handi Lazeez, **a delectable chicken from the cooking pot.

— Ingredients —

Boneless chicken thighs
— *800 gms*
Cardamoms — *4*
Chicken stock
— *½ litre/2 cups*
Cinnamon — *1" stick*
Cloves — *10*
Salt to taste

Refined oil
— *75 ml/5 tbs*
Garlic paste
— *20 gms/4 tsp*
Garlic, chopped
— *30 gms/2 tbs*
Ginger paste — *20 gms/4 tsp*
Onions, sliced
— *90 gms/1/3 cup*
Saffron — *1 gm/a pinch*
Yellow chilli powder
— *2.5 gms/½ tsp*

— Steps —

1. Cut chicken into bite-sized pieces.
2. Soak saffron in a little water in a spoon for 10 minutes. Crush and keep aside.
3. Heat oil in a saucepan and add chopped garlic. Sauté till brown.
4. Add the onions and sauté till light brown.
5. Add cinnamon, cloves and cardamoms and sauté till the onions turn golden brown.
6. Add the ginger and garlic pastes, chicken, salt and yellow chilli powder. Stir for 3-4 minutes.
7. Add chicken stock and bring to boil. Cover and simmer till chicken is tender.
8. Remove from fire. Take out the chicken

pieces from the gravy. Strain the gravy into another pot through a soup strainer.

9. Cook the gravy till reduced to a sauce-like consistency.

10. Add the chicken pieces and cook for a minute.

Time: Preparation: 20 minutes
Cooking: 30 minutes

To serve: Stir in the prepared saffron. Serve hot with an Indian bread of your choice.

BUTTER CHICKEN

SERVES: 4

A rich, roast chicken delicacy, favourite among north Indians, locally known as Murgh Makhani..

— Ingredients —

Pre-cooked tandoori chicken (cut into 8 pieces each) — *2*

Bay leaf (*tej patta*)— *1*

Butter — *120 gms/²/₃ cup*

Cinnamon sticks — *2*

Cream — *150 ml/³/₄ cup*

Garlic paste — *50 gms/3¹/₃ tbs*

Ginger juliennes — *10 gms/2 tsp*

Ginger paste — *50 gms/3¹/₃ tbs*

Green cardamoms — *10*

Green chillies (slit and deseeded) — *5*

Honey — *1 tbs*

Green coriander, chopped
— *15 gms/3 tsp*
Paprika or red chilli powder
— *5 gms/1 tsp*
Salt to taste
Tomatoes, chopped
— *900 gms/4½ cups*
Water — *200 ml/1 cup*

— *Steps* —

1. Melt half the butter in a thick bottom pan, sauté the cinnamon, cardamoms and bay leaf for 30 seconds, stir in the ginger and garlic pastes, and cook till the water evaporates.

2. Add tomatoes and salt and cook till the tomatoes dissolve. Add 2 cups of water and let it simmer for some time.

3. Strain the gravy through a soup strainer into another pan.

4. Melt the remaining butter in a kadhai/wok, add the ginger juliennes and green chillies. Sauté for a minute.

5. Add the paprika—the colour of the mixture will turn a bright red.

6. Add the strained gravy and bring to a boil.

7. Add the tandoori chicken pieces. Simmer for 10 minutes till the chicken gets soft. Stir in the cream and honey.

TIPS

Time: Preparation: 20 minutes+time to roast the chicken.
Cooking: 25 minutes

To serve: Serve garnished with green coriander and accompanied by any Indian bread.

SAAG CHICKEN

SERVES: 4

Chicken curried in a spicy spinach purée.

— Ingredients —

Chicken, skinned and cut into pieces — *1 kg*
Bay leaves (*tej patta*) — *2*
Butter — *100 gms/½ cup*
Cinnamon sticks — *4*
Fenugreek leaves powder (*methi*) — *3 gms/²/₃ tsp*
Garlic paste — *40 gms/2²/₃ tbs*
Ginger juliennes — *10 gms/2 tsp*
Ginger paste — *40 gms/2²/₃ tbs*
Oil — *60 ml/4 tbs*

Maize flour (*makki ka atta*) — *3 gms/²/₃ tsp*
Onion paste — *200 gms/1 cup*
Red chilli powder — *10 gms/2 tsp*
Salt to taste
Spinach (*palak*), puréed — *350 gms/1¾ cups*
Tomatoes, chopped — *180 gms/¾ cup*
Water — *40 ml/2²/₃ tbs*
White pepper powder — *3 gms/²/₃ tsp*

— Steps —

1. Heat oil in a pan, add the whole spices (cinnamon and bay leaves), and sauté over medium heat until they begin to crackle.

2. Add ginger, garlic, onion pastes and red chilli powder. Sauté for 30-60 seconds. Add tomatoes and sauté further for 1 minute.

3. Add spinach purée, stir in maize flour diluted with water. Cook over medium heat for 10-15 minutes, stirring occasionally.

4. In another pan heat the butter and sauté the chicken.

5. Transfer the chicken pieces into the spinach sauce.

6. Add salt and white pepper powder, cover and simmer on very low heat till chicken is cooked.

TIPS

Time: Preparation: 10 minutes
Cooking: 45 minutes

To serve: Serve garnished with ginger juliennes and fenugreek powder.

AFGHANI CHICKEN

SERVES: 4

Creamy chicken curry.

— Ingredients —

Chicken (boneless) — *800 gms*	Sesame seeds — *1 tsp/10 gms*
Yoghurt — *1 cup/225 gms*	Nutmeg powder — *½ tsp/2 gms*
Ginger paste — *4 tsp/60 gms*	Oil — *8 tbs/100 ml*
Garlic paste — *2 tsp/30 gms*	Green cardamom — *2 sticks*
Onions — *2/150 gms*	Bayleaf (*tej patta*) — *2*
Red chilli powder — *1 tsp/5 gms*	Green coriander — *½ cup/20 gms*
Cashewnut paste — *½ cup/75 gms*	Salt to taste

— Steps —

1. Mix ginger paste, garlic paste, sliced onions, red chilli powder, cashewnut paste, sesame seeds, nutmeg and salt with yoghurt and marinate the chicken for 30 minutes.

2. Heat oil in a thick bottom pan. Add whole spices and stir fry till they change colour.

3. Add chicken along with marinade, bring to a boil and simmer for 5 minutes.

4. Add 400 ml water and boil for 3 minutes. Cook till chicken is tender and gravy thickens.

5. Adjust seasoning.

TIPS

Time: Preparation: ½ hour
Cooking: 20 minutes

To serve: Remove to a dish, garnish with coriander and serve with rice.

CHICKEN SHAHJAHANI

SERVES: 4

A chicken recipe from the kitchens of the Mughal emperors.

— Ingredients —

Chicken, skinned and cut into 8 pieces — *1 kg*
Bay leaves (*tej patta*) — *2*
Black cardamom powder — *3 gms/²/₃ tsp*
Black cumin (*shah jeera*) — *3 gms/²/₃ tsp*
Cashewnut paste — *100 gms/¹/₂ cup*
Cinnamon sticks (1 cm) — *3*
Coriander, chopped — *15 gms/3 tsp*
Eggs (boiled and quartered) — *3*
Garlic paste — *25 gms/5 tsp*
Ginger juliennes — *5 gms/1 tsp*

Ginger paste — *25 gms/5 tsp*
Green cardamoms — *8*
Hot water — *200 ml/1 cup*
Onions, chopped — *200 gms/1 cup*
Turmeric powder (*haldi*) — *6 gms/1¹/₃ tsp*
Yellow chilli powder — *8 gms/1²/₃ tsp*
Yoghurt, whisked — *150 gms/³/₄ cup*
Oil — *80 ml/5¹/₃ tbs*
Cream — *40 ml/2²/₃ tbs*
Cloves — *8*
Salt to taste

— Steps —

1. Heat the oil in a heavy thick bottomed pan over medium heat. Add the bay leaves, cinnamon sticks, green cardamoms, black cumin and cloves, and sauté until the spices begin to crackle.
2. Add onions, turmeric powder and yellow chilli powder, and sauté for 30 seconds.
3. Add ginger, garlic and cashewnut pastes and sauté

for 30 seconds more.

4. Add chicken pieces and cook for 10-15 minutes over medium heat.

5. Add whisked yoghurt with 2 cups of hot water and salt. Cover and simmer for 10-15 minutes on a very low heat.

6. Add the cream and cardamom powder and stir.

TIPS

Time: Preparation: 15 minutes
Cooking: 45 minutes

To serve: Serve garnished with the eggs, green coriander and ginger juliennes.

CHICKEN STUFFED WITH NUTS

SERVES: 4

A rich and creamy dish, locally known as Murgh Musallam.

— Ingredients —

Chicken, whole, skinned — 900 gms

Almond paste — 15 gms/3 tsp

Almonds, fried — 25 gms/5 tsp

Black pepper powder — 6 gms/1¹/₃ tsp

Cinnamon sticks — 4

Cloves — 10

Coriander powder — 10 gms/2 tsp

Cream — 30 ml/2 tbs

Fennel seeds (*saunf*) — 10 gms/2 tsp

Fresh coconut paste — 150 gms/³/₄ cup

Gram flour (*besan*) — 100 gms/¹/₂ cup

Green cardamoms — 8

Green coriander, chopped — 8 gms/1²/₃ tsp

Nutmeg (*jaiphal*) — 3 gms/²/₃ tsp

Oil — 100 ml/¹/₂ cup

Onion paste — 160 gms/³/₄ cup

Salt to taste

Poppy seed paste — 15 gms/3 tsp

Red chilli powder — 10 gms/2 tsp

Saffron — 1 gm

Silver leaves (*varq*) — 1

Vetivier (*kewda*) — 2 drops

Yoghurt — 200 gms/1 cup

For the stuffing:

Almonds — 100 gms/¹/₂ cup

Chicken, minced — 800 gms

Cognac (optional) — 45 ml/3 tbs

Cream — 20 ml/4 tsp

Ginger paste — 5 gms/1 tsp

Green chilli paste — 6 gms/1¹/₃ tsp

Pistachios — 25 gms/5 tsp

Mace (*javitri*) — 3 gms/²/₃ tsp

Raisins — 15 gms/3 tsp

Salt to taste

— Steps —

1. In a bowl combine all the ingredients for the stuffing. Fill it into the stomach cavity of the dressed chicken.

2. In a pan, heat the oil and fry the stuffed chicken until it is golden brown. Keep aside.

3. In the same pan add cardamoms, fennel seeds, cinnamon sticks, cloves and onion paste. Sauté for 30-60 seconds. Add red chilli powder, black pepper, salt and coriander powder. Cook over low heat for 5-10 minutes.

4. Add poppy seed paste, almond paste, coconut paste and 2 cups of hot water and bring to a boil.

5. Add the chicken, cover and cook on a low heat until the chicken is cooked.

6. Remove the chicken and strain the sauce and add saffron, cream, nutmeg and kewda to the sauce.

TIPS

Time: Preparation: 25 minutes
Cooking: 45 minutes

To serve: Place chicken on a serving dish. Pour the sauce over the chicken and garnish with almonds, silver leaves and green coriander leaves.

Murgh Begam-Bahar

SERVES: 4

Chicken curry garnished with lamb.

— Ingredients —

Chicken — *1 kg*
Bay leaves (*tej patta*) — *2*
Butter — *20 gms/4 tsp*
Cashewnut paste
— *100 gms/¹/₂ cup*
Cinnamon sticks (1 cm) — *3*
Cloves — *8*
Cream — *80 ml/5¹/₃ tbs*
Fenugreek (*methi*) powder
— *2 gms/¹/₂ tsp*
Garam masala
— *15 gms/3 tsp*
Garlic paste — *25 gms/5 tsp*
Ginger paste — *25 gms/5 tsp*
Green cardamoms — *8*
Green coriander, chopped
— *15 gms/3 tsp*
Hot water — *30 ml/2 tbs*

Lamb brain (parboiled)
— *100 gms/¹/₂ cup*
Salt — *15 gms/3 tsp*
Oil — *80 ml/5¹/₃ tbs*
Onions, chopped
— *200 gms/1 cup*
Red chilli powder
— *8 gms/1²/₃ tsp*
Turmeric powder (*haldi*)
— *6 gms/1¹/₃ tsp*
Yoghurt, whisked
— *150 gms/³/₄ cup*
For parboiling the brain:
Water — *¹/₂ litre*
Salt — *10 gms/2 tsp*
Turmeric (*haldi*)
— *5 gms/1 tsp*

— Steps —

1. Clean and skin the chicken and cut into 8 pieces.
2. Heat oil in a heavy bottomed pan over medium heat. Add bay leaves, cinnamon sticks, green cardamoms and cloves and sauté till they crackle.
3. Add the chopped onions, turmeric powder and red chilli powder and sauté for another 30 seconds.
4. Add the ginger and garlic pastes and cashewnut paste, and sauté for another 30 seconds.
5. Add the chicken pieces, stir and cook for 10-15 minutes on medium heat. Add salt and yoghurt.
6. Add hot water. Cover and simmer for 10 minutes on low heat. Add cream, garam masala and fenugreek powder.
7. For parboiling the brain, bring the water to boil along with the salt and turmeric.
8. Add lamb brain and lower the heat. Once the brain

rises to the top, remove it from the pan and keep aside.

9. In other pan, heat the butter. Sauté the lamb brain for 2-3 minutes. Break it up with the help of a spoon.

Time: Preparation: 15 minutes
Cooking: 30 minutes

To serve: Garnish with the fried brain and chopped green coriander.

KESARI CHICKEN

SERVES: 4

Succulent chicken in a saffron gravy.

— Ingredients —

Chicken (boneless, cut into 8 pcs) — *800 gms*
Cashewnut paste — *75 gms*
Boiled onion paste — *160 gms*
Saffron — *1 gm*
Ginger paste — *30 gms*
Garlic paste — *30 gms*
Cream — *150 ml*
Cloves — *6*

Coriander powder — *6 gms*
Salt to taste
Oil — *100 ml*
Yoghurt — *225 gms*
Bay leaf (*tej patta*)— *2*
Cardamom — *6*
White pepper powder — *1 tsp/3 gms*

— Steps —

1. Heat oil in a thick bottom pan. Add bay leaf, cloves and cardamom and stir until cardamom changes colour.
2. Add boiled onion paste, ginger and garlic paste and stir fry till oil appears on surface.
3. Add coriander powder and cashewnut paste and stir fry for 2 minutes.
4. Add boneless chicken and fry for 3 minutes.
5. Whisk in the yoghurt, add salt, pepper powder and saffron. Bring to boil. Simmer until chicken is tender.

Time: Preparation: 20 minutes
Cooking: 35 minutes

To serve: Finish with cream. Serve with hot Indian bread.

CHICKEN NAVRATTAN KORMA

SERVES: 4

A rich curry garnished with dried fruits!

— Ingredients —

Chicken boneless or chicken with bone, cut into 8 pieces — *1 kg*

Almond paste — *100 gms/° cup*

Bay leaf (*tej patta*) — *1*

Butter, unsalted — *25 gms/5 tsp*

Cinnamon sticks — *5*

Cloves — *6*

Cream — *120 ml/²/₃ cup*

Garlic paste — *30 gms/6 tsp*

Ginger paste — *30 gms/6 tsp*

Green cardamoms — *10*

Green chillies, slit into half — *6*

Mace powder (*javitri*) — *3 gms/²/₃ tsp*

Onions, grated — *180 gms/∫ cup*

Red chilli powder — *10 gms/2 tsp*

Refined oil — *25 ml/1²/₃ tbs*

18

Salt to taste	Cashewnuts — *20 gms/4 tsp*
Turmeric powder (*haldi*)	Fresh ginger juliennes
— *5 gms/1 tsp*	— *1 gm/˘ tsp*
Vetivier (*kewda*)	Fresh mint leaves
— *3 drops*	— *3 gms/²/₃ tsp*
Yoghurt, whisked	Hazelnuts — *10 gms/2 tsp*
— *20 gms/4 tsp*	Pistachios — *15 gms/3 tsp*
For garnishing:	Raisins — *10 gms/2 tsp*
Almonds — *20 gms/4 tsp*	Saffron strands, dissolved in
Black cumin seed (*shah*	15 ml of warm milk
jeera), roasted and	— *3 gms/²/₃ tsp*
powdered — *3 gms/²/₃ tsp*	

— Steps —

1. Fry the pistachios, cashewnuts, hazelnuts and almonds in a little butter for the garnish and keep aside.

2. Heat the oil and butter in the same pan. Add the bay leaf, cinnamon sticks, cloves and cardamoms, and sauté over medium heat until the spices begin to crackle.

3. Add the onions, and sauté for few minutes. Add the ginger and garlic pastes, turmeric and red chilli powder, almond paste, salt and whisked yoghurt, and cook over medium heat for 5-10 minutes until the oil separates from the mixture.

4. Add the chicken, stir and cook over medium heat for 20-25 minutes till the chicken is cooked.

5. Add cream, green chillies, mace powder and few drops of vetivier.

TIPS

Time: Preparation: 15 minutes
Cooking: 40 minutes

To serve: Garnish with sautéed nuts, raisins, ginger juliennes and saffron. Sprinkle with cumin seed powder and mint leaves, and serve hot with steamed rice or rotis.

Fried Chicken Curry

SERVES: 4

Boneless chicken pieces simmered in a spicy gravy.

— Ingredients —

Chicken — *1.2 kg*

Black peppercorns, pounded
— *2.5 gms/¹/₂ tsp*

Cardamom powder
— *2.5 gms/¹/₂ tsp*

Clove powder
— *1.25 gms/¹/₄ tsp*

Cinnamon powder
— *1.25 gms/¹/₄ tsp*

Coriander leaves, chopped
— *20 gms/4 tsp*

Coriander powder
— *2.5 gms/¹/₂ tsp*

Garlic paste — *30 gms/6 tsp*

Ginger paste — *45 gms/3 tbs*

Groundnut oil
— *80 ml/¹/₃ cup*

Lemon juice — *15 ml/3 tsp*

Onions, chopped
— *85 gms/¹/₃ cup*

Red chilli powder
— *2.5 gms/¹/₂ tsp*

Tamarind (*imlee*)
— *25 gms/5 tsp*

Curry leaves — *12*	Salt to taste
Tomatoes, chopped	Turmeric (*haldi*) powder
— *120 gms/½ cup*	— *5 gms/1 tsp*

— *Steps* —

1. Clean the chicken, debone and cut into 1½" cubes.
2. Mix red chillies, turmeric and salt with half of the ginger and garlic pastes and rub this marinade on to the chicken pieces. Keep aside for 30 minutes.
3. Heat oil in a kadhai, add the marinaded chicken and sauté over medium heat until evenly light brown.
4. Remove the chicken and reserve the oil.
5. Soak the tamarind in 25 ml/5 teaspoons water. After 10 minutes, mash well, squeeze out the pulp and discard. Keep extract aside.
6. Reheat the reserved oil, add the curry leaves and stir over low heat for 30 seconds. Add onions and sauté until light brown. Add the remaining ginger and garlic pastes, stir for a minute, add tomatoes and stir. Cook till the fat appears on the sides of the pan. Add the cardamom, coriander, clove and cinnamon powders, and stir for a minute. Add the tamarind and cook for 5 minutes.
7. Add the chicken pieces and simmer for 8-10 minutes. Add 240 ml/1 cup water and bring to boil. Reduce to medium heat and cook, stirring constantly until the moisture has evaporated and the masala coats the chicken pieces.
8. Sprinkle with pepper and lemon juice.

TIPS

Time:
Preparation: 1 hour
Cooking: 45 minutes

To serve: Remove to a flat dish, garnish with green coriander and serve with dosa and paratha.

MURGH-E-KHAS

SERVES: 4

Chicken kebabs stuffed with nuts.

— Ingredients —

Chicken legs, whole — *4*
Chicken, minced — *300 gms*
Almonds — *50 gms/3¹/₃ tbs*
Cashewnuts
— *50 gms/3¹/₃ tbs*
Cream — *100 ml/½ cup*
Garam masala — *5 gms/1 tsp*
Garlic paste — *25 gms/5 tsp*
Ginger paste — *25 gms/5 tsp*

Salt to taste
Green chilli paste
— *25 gms/5 tsp*
Groundnut oil — *15 ml/3 tsp*
Lemon juice — *30 ml/2 tbs*
Mint chutney
— *100 gms/½ cup*
Saffron — *1 gm*

— Steps —

1. Debone the entire chicken leg, leaving only the top of the drumstick. Flatten the chicken leg using a steak hammer.

2. Make a marinade with half the quantity of ginger and garlic paste, salt, green chilli paste and lemon juice. Marinate the chicken in this and refrigerate for ½ hour.

3. Chop the almonds and cashewnuts and mix with the chicken mince and chutney.

4. Add garam masala and the remaining ginger, garlic, green chilli pastes, salt and lemon juice to the mince mixture and mix well.

5. Stuff the deboned chicken with this mixture, rolling chicken in such a way that the mince is wrapped in it.

6. Grease a baking tray with oil. Place the rolls on the tray and cover with foil. Bake in a medium oven, 100 °C (200 °F) until done (approximately 20 minutes).

7. Take the chicken out and remove the foil. Slice each chicken roll diagonally and arrange on a platter. Pour the saffron mixed with cream over the sliced chicken.

TIPS

Time: Preparation: 45 minutes
Cooking: 20 minutes

To serve: Serve hot, garnished with lemon wedges and tomato slices.

TANGY CHICKEN

SERVES: 4

A rich, tart chicken dish, served with any accompaniment.

— Ingredients —

Chicken breasts — *12*
Almond paste — *45 gms/3 tbs*
Black pepper powder — *5 gms/1 tsp*
Cumin (*jeera*) seeds — *5 gms/1 tsp*
Capsicum, cut in rings — *100 gms*
Garlic paste — *20 gms/4 tsp*
Ginger paste — *20 gms/4 tsp*

Green chillies, chopped — *4*
Lemon juice — *30 ml/2 tbs*
Onions, cut in rings — *160 gms/²/₃ cup*
Saffron — *a pinch, dissolved in 1 tbs milk*
Salt to taste
White butter — *60 gms/4 tbs*
Yoghurt (drained) — *120 gms/1¼ cup*

— Steps —

1. Clean and debone chicken breasts.

2. Make a marinade of yoghurt, ginger and garlic pastes, salt, cumin, black pepper, lemon, green chillies and almond paste and marinade the chicken in it for half an hour.

3. Grease an ovenproof shallow dish. Place the chicken pieces in it, without overlapping. Arrange the onion and capsicum rings over the chicken pieces and pour the leftover marinade evenly over it.

4. Dot with dollops of remaining butter and roast in a preheated oven at 300 ºF for 20 minutes.

5. Remove, sprinkle saffron, cover and let simmer in the oven for another 10 minutes.

TIPS

Time: Preparation: 45 minutes
Cooking: 20 minutes

To serve: Uncover dish, wipe edges and serve hot with roti, raita and chutney.

PRAWN CURRY

SERVES: 4

A traditional prawn curry from south India. Seafood in India is readily available in the southern parts as most states in the south have a long coastline.

— Ingredients —

Prawns — *1 kg*
Coconut, grated — *75 gms/1 cup*
Coriander chopped — *20 gms/¹/₃ cup*
Coriander powder — *10 gms/2 tsp*
Curry leaves — *10*
Garlic paste — *20 gms/3¹/₂ tsp*
Ginger paste — *10 gms/1³/₄ tsp*
Groundnut oil — *60 ml/4 tbs*
Mustard (*raee*) seeds — *3 gms/1 tsp*
Onions, chopped — *200 gms/1¹/₄ cup*
Red chilli powder — *10 gms/2 tsp*

Salt to taste
Turmeric (*haldi*) powder — *3 gms/¹/₂ tsp*
Tomatoes, chopped — *300 gms/1¹/₃ cup*

— Steps —

1. Shell, devein, wash and pat dry prawns.
2. Put the coconut in a blender with 60 ml/¹/₄ cup of water and make a fine paste.
3. Heat the oil in a handi and crackle mustard seeds and then saute the onions over medium heat till transparent.
4. Add garlic and ginger paste. Stir and cook till

24

all liquid has evaporated.

5. Add coriander powder, red chillies, turmeric and salt. Stir.

6. Then add the tomatoes and cook till the tomatoes are mashed.

7. Reduce to low heat and add the coconut paste and the curry leaves. Stir for two minutes.

8. Add the prawns and water (approximately 400ml/ 1²/₃ cups.) Bring to a boil, reduce to low heat and simmer, stirring occasionally until prawns are cooked.

TIPS

| **Time**: Preparation: 45 minutes
Cooking: 30 minutes |

To serve: Transfer to a bowl, garnish with coriander and serve hot with boiled rice.

GOAN FISH CURRY

SERVES: 4

This traditional spicy hot curry is a regular at most Goan meals.

— Ingredients —

Pomfret darnes — *600 gms*
Coconut, grated
— *160 gms/²/₃ cups*
Coconut milk — *160 ml/²/₃ cup*
Coriander seeds
— *15 gms/1 tbs*
Cumin (*jeera*) seeds
— *5 gms/1 tsp*
Garlic paste — *5 gms/1 tsp*
Ginger paste — *20 gms/4 tsp*
Green chillies — *4*
Groundnut oil — *60 ml/¹/₄ cup*

Lemon juice — *60 ml/¹/₄ cup*
Onions, chopped
— *60 gms/¹/₄ cup*
Red chillies, whole — *15*
Salt to taste
Tamarind (*imlee*), deseeded
— *45 gms/3 tbs*
Tomatoes, chopped
— *60 gms/¹/₄ cup*
Turmeric (*haldi*) powder
— *5 gms/1 tsp*

— Steps —

1. Sprinkle salt and lemon on the fish and marinate for an hour.
2. Meanwhile blend the coconut, whole chillies, cumin seeds, coriander, turmeric, tamarind, ginger and garlic pastes together in a blender with some coconut milk.
3. Heat oil in a kadhai. Add onions and saute till golden brown. Add tomatoes and cook for 3 to 4 minutes till the tomatoes are mashed.
4. Add blended mix with water (240 ml/1 cup), and bring to a boil.
5. Add green chillies and the fish. Simmer for 7 minutes.
6. Bring to a boil and then let it simmer again for 2 minutes. Do not cover the pot at any stage while the curry is being cooked.

TIPS

Time: Preparation: 45 minutes
Cooking: 30 minutes

To serve: Remove to a bowl and serve with boiled rice.

FISH IN YOGHURT

SERVES: 4

*A **West Bengal** favourite, also known as Dahi Machchi.*

— Ingredients —

Pomfret fillets — *700 gms*
Salt to taste
Turmeric (*haldi*) — *1 tsp/5 gms*
Lemon juice — *3 tsp/45 ml*
Mustard seeds — *1tsp/3 gms*
Curry leaves — *10*
Onions (chopped) — *1/75 gms*
Ginger(chopped) — *1-2 tsp/20 gms*
Tomatoes (chopped) — *1-2/80 gms*
Yoghurt — *1 cup/150 gms*
Red chilli powder — *1 tsp/3 gms*
Cumin powder — *1 tsp/3 gms*
Coriander powder — *1 tsp/3 gms*
Oil — *8 tsp/100 ml*
Coriander leaves (for garnish)

— Steps —

1. Marinate the pomfret fillets with half the salt, lemon juice and turmeric powder.

2. Keep aside for 15 minutes and pan fry the fillets using very little oil in a nonstick pan. Keep the cooked fillets aside.

3. Take a thick bottomed pan and heat the remaining oil. Add mustard seeds and curry leaves and stir till the seeds crackle.

4. Add chopped ginger and onions and cook till onions are soft. Add tomatoes and cook till oil comes on top.

5. Add red chilli, cumin and coriander powders and the remaining turmeric. Stir for 1 minute.

6. Whisk in the yoghurt. Bring to boil and simmer for 7 minutes.

7. Slip the cooked fish into the gravy and simmer for another 4 minutes.

8. Carefully remove the fillets and place on the serving dish and pour the gravy on top.

TIPS

Time: Preparation: 20 minutes
Cooking: 25 minutes

To serve: Served garnished with chopped coriander leaves.

BAKED PRAWNS WITH POMEGRANATE

SERVES: 4

An exotic prawn dish, also known as *Jhinga Dum Anari.*

— Ingredients —

Jumbo prawns — *800 gms/8*

Cheddar cheese
— *30 gms/2 tbs*

Coriander leaves chopped
— *10 gms/2 tsp*

Cumin (*jeera*) seeds
— *2.5 gms/½ tsp*

Garlic paste — *10 gms/2 tsp*

Ginger, chopped fine
— *5 gms/1 tsp*

Ginger paste — *10 gms/2 tsp*

Lemon juice — *30 ml/2 tbs*

Malt vinegar — *30 ml/2 tbs*

Peas, fresh — *120 gms/½ cup*

Pickled onions, chopped	Tomato ketchup —45 ml/3 tbs
— 60 gms/¼ cup	White pepper powder
Pomegranate seeds	— 2.5 gms/½ tsp
(*anar dana*), fresh	Yellow chilli powder
— 240 gms/1 cup	— 2.5 gms/½ tsp
	Salt to taste

— Steps —

1. Remove the head from the prawns, slit, devein, wash and pat dry.

2. Mix malt vinegar, salt, yellow chilli powder, ginger and garlic pastes and marinade prawns in it for half an hour.

3. Place each prawn on a separate 10 inch square piece of greased aluminium foil.

4. Boil, drain and crush peas with a rolling pin.

5. Mix in cheese, onion, coriander, ginger, cumin, lemon juice, white pepper powder, tomato ketchup and pomegranate seeds.

6. Top each prawn with this mixture.

7. Grate cheese on each and wrap up the foil.

8. Place the parcels in a baking tray and bake in a preheated oven at 275 °F for 10-12 minutes.

TIPS

Time: Preparation: 45 minutes
Cooking: 15 minutes

To serve: Serve hot as a heavy snack.

MAHI MUSALLAM

SERVES: 4

A whole large fish smothered in cashewnut and fenugreek (methi).

— Ingredients —

River or sea fish (whole)
— *2 kg*
Butter, melted
— *30 gms/2 tbs*
Cashewnut paste
— *100 gms/½ cup*
Coriander powder
— *15 gms/3 tsp*
Fenugreek powder (*methi*)
— *6 gms/1⅓ tsp*
Garam masala
— *15 gms/3 tsp*
Garlic paste
— *50 gms/3⅓ tbs*
Ginger paste
— *50 gms/3⅓ tbs*
Lemon juice — *15 ml/1 tbs*

Oil — *200 ml/1 cup*
Onion paste
— *200 gms/1 cup*
Red chilli powder
— *10 gms/2 tsp*
Salt to taste
Turmeric powder (*haldi*)
— *10 gms/2 tsp*
Vetivier (*kewda*) — *5 drops*
Yoghurt — *180 gms/¾ cup*
For the marinade:
Garlic paste — *20 gms/4 tsp*
Ginger paste — *20 gms/4 tsp*
Lemon juice — *15 ml/1 tbs*
Red chilli powder
— *5 gms/1 tsp*
Salt to taste

— Steps —

1. Clean, wash and wipe the fish thoroughly.
2. Mix all the ingredients for the marinade. Prick the fish with a sharp fork, rub the marinade all over and leave aside for 1 hour.
3. Heat the oil in a pan to smoking point. Arrange the fish in a baking dish. Baste the fish with hot oil until the fish is half cooked.
4. To the oil left in the pan add onion paste, ginger and garlic pastes and cashewnut paste and stir. Add coriander powder, red chilli powder, turmeric powder and salt.

5. Add the yoghurt, bring the mixture to a boil, reduce to medium heat and stir until the oil separates from the mixture.

6. Add hot water (about 1½ cups) and bring it to a slow boil. Add fenugreek powder, garam masala and vetivier.

7. Preheat the oven to 120 °C (250 °F). Pour the hot gravy over the fish and bake for 40 minutes. At intervals of 15 minutes baste the fish with the gravy.

TIPS

Time: Preparation: 25 minutes
Cooking: 1 hour

To serve: Remove the fish gently and arrange carefully in a shallow dish. Strain the gravy and add the lemon juice. Pour the gravy over the fish and garnish with chopped green coriander and melted butter. Serve with plain rice or pooris.

FISH CURRY

SERVES: 4

*Small, fresh, sea fish in a thick brown curry with
a liberal sprinkling of whole red chillies
popular in South India.*

— Ingredients —

Pomfret/sole darnes or small
whole fresh fish — *900 gms*
Cardamoms — *2*
Cinnamon — *1" stick*
Cloves — *2*
Coconut, grated
— *120 gms/° cup*
Coriander, chopped
— *10 gms/2 tsp*

Curry leaves — *10*
Fenugreek (*methi*) seeds
— *2.5 gms/° tsp*
Groundnut oil
— *80 ml/¹/₃ cup*
Lemon juice — *30 ml/2 tbs*
Mustard (*sarson*) seeds
— *5 gms/1 tsp*
Oil to fry fish

Onions, sliced
— *80 gms/¹/₃ cup*
Red chillies, whole — 6
Salt to taste
Tamarind (*imlee*), soaked in
° cup water — *25 gms/5 tsp*
Tomatoes, chopped
— *120 gms/° cup*
Turmeric (*haldi*) powder
— *5 gms/1 tsp*

— *Steps* —

1. Apply lemon juice to fish and leave for half an hour. Then wash with fresh water, squeeze lightly and pat dry. Fry the fish lightly in oil and set aside.

2. In a small pot heat 1 tablespoon/15 ml groundnut oil. Add mustard seeds, fenugreek seeds, cardamoms, cinnamon, cloves, whole red chillies and sauté lightly then cool. Blend to a smooth paste in a blender with the grated coconut.

3. Mash the soaked tamarind with your fingers, then squeeze out and discard the pulp. Keep the extract aside.

4. Heat the rest of the groundnut oil in a pot and sauté onions till brown. Add the tomatoes and turmeric and stircook for 4 to 5 minutes. Add the tamarind extract and bring to a boil, reduce flame and let simmer for another 5 minutes.

5. Add coconut paste to the gravy. Cook till gravy thickens. Add salt and curry leaves.

6. Gently add the fried fish to the curry and simmer for 5 minutes.

TIPS

Time: Preparation: 30 minutes
Cooking: 30 minutes

To serve: Garnish with fresh coriander leaves and serve hot with boiled rice or roti

PICKLED LAMB CHOPS

SERVES: 4

Lamb chops cooked with whole spices.

— Ingredients —

Lamb chops, on 2 bones — *8 pieces*	Mustard oil (*sarson ka tel*) — *50 ml/3¹/₃ tbs*
Aniseed — *5 gms/1 tsp*	Mustard seeds (*raee*) — *5 gms/1 tsp*
Black cardamom — *2 gms/¹/₂ tsp*	Onion seeds (*kalonji*) — *5 gms/1 tsp*
Black pepper — *5 gms/1 tsp*	Raw papaya, a small piece,
Chaat masala — *5 gms/1 tsp*	or meat tenderizer
Cloves — *3 gms/²/₃ tsp*	Red chilli powder
Garlic paste — *10 gms/2 tsp*	— *15 gms/3 tsp*
Ginger paste — *10 gms/2 tsp*	Yoghurt, whisked
Gram flour (*besan*) — *10 gms/2 tsp*	— *50 gms/¹/₄ cup*
Lemon juice — *15 ml/1 tbs*	Salt to taste

— Steps —

1. Flatten the chops with a steak hammer.
2. Rub the chops with the papaya, ginger and garlic pastes and salt and keep aside.
3. Heat the gram flour in a pan till light brown and sprinkle over the lamb chops.
4. To the yoghurt add the remaining ingredients and

LAMB WITH WHOLE SPICE

SERVES: 4

An aromatic lamb dish laced with the flavour of crackled whole spices, also known as Handi Pasinda.

— Ingredients —

Lamb escallops (2" x 4") — *750 gms*

Bay leaf (*tej patta*) — *1*

Black cardamoms — *2*

Black pepper powder — *2.5 gms/½ tsp*

Cardamom powder — *2.5 gms/½ tsp*

Cinnamon — *1" stick*

Cloves — *6*

Cooking oil — *120 ml/½ cup*

Coriander leaves, chopped — *5 gms/1 tsp*

Garam masala — *5 gms/1 tsp*

Garlic cloves — *45 gms/3 tbs*

Ginger — *25 gms/1 sq" piece*

Onions, sliced — *240 gms/1 cups*

Poppy seeds — *15 gms/1 tbs*

Red chilli powder — *5 gms/1 tsp*

Yoghurt — *240 gms/1 cup*

— *Steps* —

1. Heat oil in a kadhai and sauté half the onions till golden brown. Remove.

2. Peel and chop the ginger and the garlic. Mix with the browned and raw onions and poppy seeds and blend to a fine paste with 30 ml/2 tbs water.

3. Heat the oil left in the kadhai and crackle the black cardamoms, cinnamon, bay leaf and cloves. Add blended paste and sauté for 3 to 4 minutes.

4. Add yoghurt and cook for 4 to 5 minutes. Add the lamb pieces and cook for another 3-4 minutes till the fat surfaces.

5. Transfer to a casserole. Add 120 ml/½ cup water.

6. Sprinkle red chilli powder, garam masala, cardamom powder and black pepper powder on top. Cover and cook in a preheated oven at 275 °F for 10 minutes.

TIPS

Time: Preparation: 30 minutes
Cooking: 45 minutes

To serve: Garnish with coriander, wipe the edges of the dish and serve with naan.

KOHE AWADH

SERVES: 4

A lamb curry with a difference.

— Ingredients —

Lamb meat from the shanks, on the bone (*kareli*) — 1 kg/10 pieces
Bay leaves (*tej patta*) — 2
Black pepper powder — 5 gms/1 tsp
Cinnamon sticks — 2
Cloves — 8
Cumin powder (*jeera*) — 1 gm/$^1/_5$ tsp

Garlic paste — 40 gms/$2^2/_3$ tbs
Ghee (clarified butter) — 60 ml/$^1/_3$ cup
Ginger juliennes — 10 gms/2 tsp
Ginger paste — 40 gms/$2^2/_3$ tbs
Green cardamoms — 8

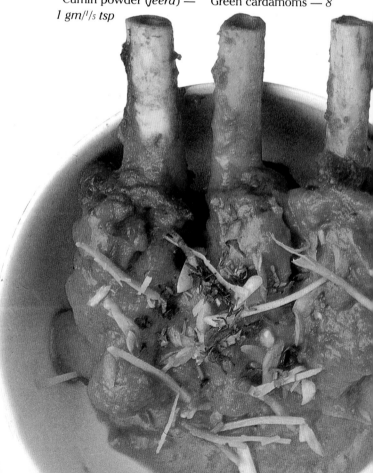

Green coriander, chopped — *5 gms/1 tsp*	Mace powder (*javitri*) — *5 gms/1 tsp*
Green cardamom powder — *1 gm/¹/₅ tsp*	Milk — *15 ml/1 tbs*
	Onions — *175 gms/¾ cup*
Kashmiri red chilli powder — *5 gms/1 tsp*	Saffron — *5 gms/1 tsp*
	Vetivier (*kewda*) — *2 drops*
Salt to taste	Yoghurt — *400 gms/2 cups*

— Steps —

1. Fry the onions in a little ghee, grind to a paste, and keep aside.

2. In the same pan, heat the rest of the ghee and add the meat, green cardamoms, cloves, cinnamon, bay leaves, ginger and garlic paste, and salt. Cover and cook on low heat for 30 minutes. Stir occasionally. Uncover and stir fry for a few minutes until the liquid evaporates.

3. Add the yoghurt and continue to stir fry till the liquid evaporates again.

4. Add the red chilli powder, dissolved in 30 ml of water, and stir for a minute. Add the fried onion paste dissolved in 3 tbs of water and continue to fry. Add a tablespoon of water when the liquid evaporates, to ensure that the sauce and lamb do not burn.

5. Add half the pepper and cumin and 6 cups of water and bring to a boil. Cover, lower the heat, seal the lid with dough and simmer on *dum* for at least 1 hour.

6. Unseal and remove the lamb from the gravy. Strain the gravy, return to the stove and reduce the gravy to pouring consistency.

7. Add the mace, cardamom powder and the saffron with kewda mixed in milk. Cook for about 5 minutes.

TIPS

Time: Preparation: 15 minutes
Cooking: 3 hours

To serve: Pour sauce over the *kareli*. Garnish with ginger juliennes and green coriander.

Nahari Gosht

SERVES: 4

A favourite of the Nawabs of Lucknow.

— Ingredients —

Lamb with bone (any cut) — 1 kg	Coriander powder — 20 gms/4 tsp
Bay leaves (*tej patta*) — 2	Fennel powder (*saunf*) — 4 gms/³⁄₄ tsp
Black pepper — 20	
Cinnamon sticks — 4	Flour — 4 gms/³⁄₄ tsp
Cloves — 10	Garam masala — 10 gms/2 tsp

Garlic paste — *5 gms/1 tsp*	Onions, chopped
Ginger paste — *5 gms/1 tsp*	— *250 gms/1¼ cups*
Gram flour (*besan*)	Onions, sliced
— *4 gms/¾ tsp*	— *250 gms/1¼ cups*
Green cardamoms — *10*	Red chillies — *10 gms/8*
Green coriander, chopped	Saffron — *1 gm*
— *15 gms/3 tsp*	Turmeric powder (*haldi*)
Lemon juice — *10 ml/2 tsp*	— *10 gms/2 tsp*
Mace (*javitri*) — *3 gms/²/₃ tsp*	Vetivier (*kewda*) — *1 tbs*
Mustard oil (*sarson ka tel*)	Yoghurt, whisked
— *150 ml/½ cup*	— *200 gms/1 cup*
Salt to taste	

— *Steps* —

1. Clean and cut lamb into small pieces with the bone.

2. Heat 100 ml (½ cup) oil in a kadhai/wok, add the sliced onions and sauté over medium heat until golden brown.

3. Add the lamb, chopped onions, green cardamoms, cloves, cinnamon, black pepper and bay leaves and cook until the liquid evaporates.

4. Add coriander powder, red chillies, turmeric, ginger and garlic pastes and salt and cook until the oil separates from the mixture.

5. Add the yoghurt, bring to a boil, reduce to medium heat and cook for 10 minutes.

6. Add 1 litre water and bring to a boil again. Cover and simmer, stirring occasionally, until lamb is tender.

7. Remove the meat from the gravy and keep aside.

8. Heat 3 tbs of the oil in a pan, add the flour and gram flour and cook over low heat, stirring constantly, until light brown. Add the gravy and stir.

9. Pass the thickened gravy through a soup strainer, return to the fire and bring to a boil.

10. Add the lamb, garam masala, fennel powder, lemon juice, vetivier, saffron and the mace, and stir.

TIPS

Time: Preparation: 15 minutes
Cooking: 45 minutes

To serve: Serve, garnished with green coriander leaves, with Indian bread.

LAMB ROGAN JOSH

SERVES: 4

A mild Kashmiri lamb dish.

— Ingredients —

Lamb (preferably chops) — *1 kg*
Bay leaves (*tej patta*) — *3*
Black cumin seeds (*shah jeera*) — *2 gms/½ tsp*
Cinnamon sticks — *2*
Cloves — *10*
Fennel seed powder (*saunf*) — *5 gms/1 tsp*
Salt to taste

Ginger paste — *10 gms/2 tsp*
Green cardamoms — *8*
Onions, chopped — *180 gms/¾ cups*
Red chilli powder — *10 gms/2 tsp*
Refined oil — *60 ml/4 tbs*
Sugar — *5 gms/1 tsp*
Tomatoes, skinned, deseeded and chopped — *400 gms/2 cups*
Water/ lamb stock — *200 ml/1 cup*

— Steps —

1. Clean lamb chops and remove excess fat. Pat with a paper towel, sprinkle with salt, and keep aside for 10 minutes.
2. Heat the oil, add sugar, cloves, bay leaves, green cardamoms and cinnamon sticks. Sauté for 2-3 minutes.
3. Add the lamb chops and cook over medium heat until the lamb chops are lightly browned.
4. Add the chopped onions and sauté till browned.
5. Add red chilli powder, black cumin seeds, chopped tomatoes and ginger paste and fry till oil separates from the gravy.
6. Add the water/stock and cook until the chops are tender.
7. Add fennel seed powder. Cover and simmer for 10 minutes on a low fire.

TIPS

Time: Preparation: 15 minutes Cooking: 35 minutes
To serve: Serve, garnished with a pinch of fennel seed powder, with steamed rice or roti.

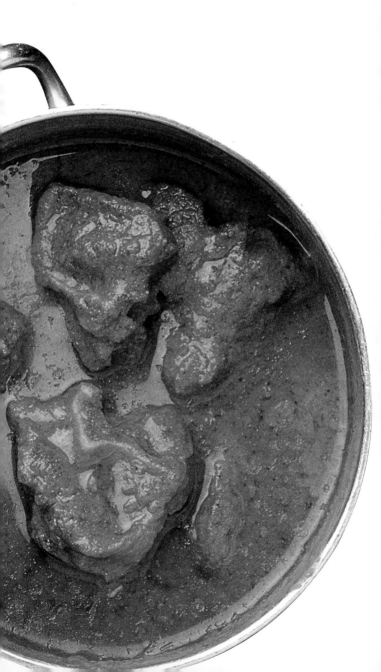

KARELI KA ROGAN JOSH

SERVES: 4

Lamb cooked in a smooth gravy and simmered in an oven.

— Ingredients —

Lamb shins — *800 gms/8*
Almond paste — *15 gms/1 tbs*
Cardamoms — *5*
Chilli powder — *5 gms/1 tsp*
Cloves — *3*
Coriander leaves, chopped
— *10 gms/1 tbs*
Garam masala
— *2.5 gms/½ tsp*
Garlic paste — *30 gms/2 tbs*
Ginger juliennes
— *5 gms/1 tsp*

Ginger paste — *30 gms/2 tbs*
Oil — *20 gms/4 tsp*
Onion paste, browned
— *30 gms/2 tbs*
Saffron — *a pinch*
Salt to taste
Stock — *750 ml/3 cups*
Sweet ittar — *a few drops*
Tomato purée
— *120 gms/½ cup*
Yoghurt — *45 gms/3 tbs*

— Steps —

1. Heat the oil, crackle the cloves and cardamoms, add ginger and garlic pastes and sauté till almost dry.
2. Add lamb shins, salt, yoghurt, browned onion paste and chilli powder. Stir for 3-5 minutes. Add stock and simmer till meat is tender.
3. Remove shins into an ovenproof casserole and strain the curry into another pan.
4. Add tomato purée to the strained curry and cook till only two-thirds of the liquid is left.
5. Stir in the almond paste and the garam masala. Cook for 2-3 minutes. Pour over the cooled shins.
6. Sprinkle with ginger juliennes, chopped coriander, saffron (crushed in a few drops of water) and sweet ittar. Seal the casserole and let simmer for 5 minutes in a preheated oven.

TIPS

Time: Preparation: 30 minutes
Cooking: 2 hours

To serve: Open the seal and wipe edges of dish. Serve hot with taftan.

LAMB NILGIRI KORMA CURRY

SERVES: 4

Delicately spiced lamb cooked with spinach.

— Ingredients —

Lamb (boneless) — *800 gms*	Oil — *8 litre/100 ml*
Cardamom — *8*	Onions — *2-3/250 gms*
Cashewnut — *½ cup/80 gms*	Peppercorns — *10*
Cloves — *6*	Poppy seeds — *3 tbs/20 gms*
Ginger paste — *2 tbs/40 gms*	Salt to taste
Green coriander	Spinach — *300 gms*
— *1 cup/200 gms*	Tomatoes — *2/125 gms*
Mint (fresh)	Yellow chilli powder
— *½ cup/100 gms*	— *1 tbs/10 gms*

— Steps —

1. Wash and clean, coriander, mint and spinach. Blanch the spinach in salted boiling water for 1½ minute.
2. Cool and make a fine puree in blender along with coriander and mint. Keep aside.
3. Cut lamb into 1 inch cubes keep aside.
4. Soak poppy seeds and cashewnut in hot water for 30 minutes. Blend and make a fine paste. Keep aside.
5. Heat oil in a thick bottom pan. Crackle cardamoms and cloves.
6. Add onion paste, ginger, garlic paste and stir fry for 5-6 minutes. Add lamb cubes and stir fry till lamb is evenly seared.
7. Add chopped tomatoes, yellow chilli powder, pepper corns and salt. Stir fry for 2 minutes. Add 200 ml of water and bring to a boil and simmer till water evaporates.
8. Add poppy seeds and cashewnut paste and the pureed greens. Simmer till lamb is cooked. Season and adjust consistency by adding hot water.

TIPS

Time: Preparation: 1 hour
Cooking: 45 minutes

To serve: Serve with boiled rice or hot Indian breads.

LAMB DO PIAZA

SERVES: 4

*Lamb curry with lots of onions, added twice,
hence 'do piaza'!*

— Ingredients —

Lamb, cubed — *1 kg*
Bay leaves (*tej patta*) — *3*
Black pepper crushed
— *10 gms/2 tsp*
Button onions
— *300 gms/1½ cups*
Butter — *20 gms/1⅓ tbs*
Cinnamon sticks — *5*
Cloves — *10*
Coriander powder
— *10 gms/2 tsp*

Cumin powder (*jeera*)
— *6 gms/1⅓ tsp*
Garam masala
— *12 gms/2½ tsp*
Garlic paste — *60 gms/4 tbs*
Ginger juliennes
— *6 gms/1⅓ tsp*
Ginger paste — *60 gms/4 tbs*
Green cardamom pods — *10*
Green coriander, chopped
— *5 gms/1 tsp*

Mace powder (*javitri*) — *3 gms/²/₃ tsp*	Salt to taste
Nutmeg powder (*jaiphal*) — *½ nutmeg*	Tomatoes, skinned, deseeded and chopped
Onions, chopped or sliced — *200 gms/1 cup*	— *300 gms/1½ cups*
Red chillies, whole — *10 gms/8*	Turmeric powder (*haldi*)
Refined oil — *100 ml/1 cup*	— *6 gms/1¹/₃ tsp*

— *Steps* —

1. Blanch the button onions and toss in hot butter for a few minutes.

2. Heat the oil in a pan, add the turmeric and the whole spices (bay leaves, cloves, cinnamon sticks, whole red chillies, and cardamoms) and sauté over medium heat for few seconds until they begin to crackle.

3. Add the onions and sauté until soft and golden in colour. Add the ginger and garlic pastes and chopped tomatoes, stir and cook for 5 minutes.

4. Then add the lamb, stir and cook for 10-15 minutes over medium heat until a pleasant aroma comes from the lamb. Reduce heat, simmer on a low fire and cook until the lamb is tender.

5. Sprinkle with garam masala, coriander powder, cumin powder, mace powder, nutmeg powder and black pepper powder. Adjust the salt. Add the button onions, stir, cover and cook for 2-3 minutes.

TIPS

Time: Preparation: 15 minutes
Cooking: 45 minutes

To serve: Serve sprinkled with green coriander and ginger juliennes.

Mattar Makhana Korma

SERVES: 4

*Green peas and puffed lotus seeds cooked in
green chilly and yoghurt curry.*

— Ingredients —

Green peas — *600 gms*
Puffed lotus seeds
(*makhana*) — *200 gms/1 cup*
Bay leaf (*tej patta*) — *1*
Butter — *10 gms/2 tsp*
Cashewnut paste
— *100 gms/½ cup*
Cinnamon sticks — *3*
Cloves — *10*
Cream — *60 ml/4 tbs*
Garlic paste
— *40 gms/2²/₃ tbs*
Ginger juliennes
— *5 gms/1 tsp*
Ginger paste
— *40 gms/2²/₃ tbs*
Green cardamoms — *8*
Green chilli paste
— *25 gms/5 tsp*
Green coriander, chopped
— *15 gms/3 tsp*

Oil — *60 ml/4 tbs*
Onions, chopped
— *60 gms/½ cup*
Salt to taste
White pepper — *3 gms/²/₃ tsp*
Yoghurt
— *200 gms/1 cup*

— Steps —

1. Parboil the green peas and
the *makhana*.
2. Heat the oil in a pan. Add
cloves, cinnamon sticks, bay
leaf and green cardamoms
and sauté for 30 seconds.
Add chopped onions and
sauté until golden.
3. Add the ginger and garlic
pastes, green chilli paste and

48

cashewnut paste and cook until the oil
separates from the gravy.
4. Add the yoghurt and cook on low heat for 5 minutes.
Add the peas, makhana, salt and white pepper. Cover
and cook on low heat for 5 minutes.
5. Add the cream. Lightly fry the ginger juliennes in the
butter.

VEGETARIAN

TIPS

Time: Preparation: 10 minutes
Cooking: 25 minutes

To serve: Serve garnished with ginger
juliennes and green coriander.

ZAFRANI KOFTA CURRY

SERVES: 4

An exotic curry made with cottage cheese,
eggs and saffron.

— Ingredients —

Cottage cheese (*paneer*), grated — *500 gms*
Cashewnut pieces — *50 gms/¼ cup*
Coriander powder — *25 gms/5 tsp*
Eggs — *2*
Fenugreek powder (*methi*) — *2 gms/½ tsp*
Garam masala — *3 gms/⅔ tsp*
Garlic paste — *25 gms/5 tsp*
Ghee — *100 gms/½ cup*
Ginger paste — *25 gms/5 tsp*
Green coriander, chopped — *5 gms/1 tsp*
Onions, chopped — *100 gms/½ cup*
Red chilli powder — *4 gms/¾ tsp*
Saffron (dissolved in 1 tbs milk) — *1 gm*
Salt to taste
Turmeric powder (*haldi*) — *3 gms/⅔ tsp*
White pepper powder — *2 gms/½ tsp*
Yoghurt — *100 gms/½ cup*

— Steps —

1. To the grated paneer add white pepper, cashewnut pieces, eggs and salt to taste. Divide this into 16 equal portions and make into balls.

2. Heat the ghee/butter. Deep fry the balls in hot ghee until golden. Remove from the pan.

3. In the remaining ghee add the chopped onions, garlic, ginger pastes, red chilli powder, coriander powder and turmeric powder. Cook for 10 minutes till the mixture turns brown and separates from the ghee.

4. Add garam masala, half the fenugreek powder and yoghurt and cook for about 10 minutes.

5. Add the balls very slowly to the gravy and simmer for 5 minutes.

TIPS

Time: Preparation: 15 minutes
Cooking: 45 minutes

To serve: Sprinkle with fenugreek powder, saffron dissolved in milk and chopped green coriander. Serve with naan or roti.

CASHEWNUT MUSHROOM CURRY

SERVES: 4

A mushroom curry with a nutty flavour.

— Ingredients —

Cashewnut — *20 gms/1 cup*
Mushrooms — *750 gms/3 cups*
Butter — *60 gms/ 5 tbs*
Cloves — *10*
Coriander powder — *3 gms/ 1 tsp*
Cream — *60 ml/ 5 tbs*
Cumin seeds — *4 gms*
Garlic paste — *10 gms/1 tsp*
Ginger paste — *20 gms/2 tsp*
Green coriander — *15 gms/ 2 tbs*
Mace — *3 gms*
Onions, browned — *150 gms/2 cups*
Red chilli powder — *3 gms/ 1 tsp*
Salt to taste
Tomato paste — *45 gms/3 tbs*
Turmeric (*haldi*) powder — *2 gms/½ tsp*

— Steps —

1. Soak cashewnuts in warm water for ½ an hour. Drain and keep aside. Wash mushrooms.

2. Heat butter in a thick bottom pan, add cloves, mace and cumin seeds and fry till cumin seeds begin to crackle.

3. Add ginger and garlic paste and stir fry for 1 minute. Add the browned onions and tomato paste along with the coriander, turmeric and red chilli powder. Stir fry till the butter appears on the surface.

4. Add 2 cups of water, bring to boil and simmer for 15 minutes.

5. Add mushrooms and cashewnuts and further simmer for 3 minutes. Finish with cream.

TIPS

Time: Preparation: 45 minutes
Cooking: 25 minutes

To serve: Serve hot garnished with chopped green coriander.

CURRIED AUBERGINE

SERVES: 4

Also known as Baingan ka Salan, this aubergine dish is prepared from exotic herbs and spices.

— Ingredients —

Brinjals (aubergine) — 400 gms/8 small
Coconut, desiccated — 35 gms/7 tsp
Coriander seeds — 5 gms/1 tsp
Cumin (jeera) seeds — 10 gms/2 tsp
Curry leaves — 10
Garlic paste — 10 gms/2 tsp
Ginger paste — 10 gms/2 tsp
Mustard oil (sarson ka tel) — 120 ml/½ cup
Red chilli powder — 10 gms/2 tsp
Salt to taste
Sesame (til) seeds — 10 gms/2 tsp
Tamarind (imlee) — 15 gms/3 tsp
Turmeric (haldi) powder — 5 gms/1 tsp

— Steps —

1. Roast coriander, cumin, poppy and sesame seeds on a griddle then pound. Roast coconut too.

2. Wash and soak tamarind in 240 ml/1 cup warm water. After 10 minutes, mash well, squeeze and discard pulp. Keep juice aside.

3. Slit brinjals about three-fourths of the length without separating them at the stem end.

4. Heat oil in a kadhai. Fry the brinjals lightly. Remove.

5. In the same oil brown the ginger and garlic pastes, ground spices, turmeric, red chilli powder, curry leaves and coconut.

6. Stir occasionally. Add a little water if masala begins to burn.

7. Add the brinjals and 480 ml/2 cups water. Simmer for 10 minutes.

8. Add tamarind juice through a strainer and simmer till gravy thickens.

DAAL MAKHANI

SERVES: 4

Black lentils cooked over a slow fire for hours on end are a favourite with almost all gourmets. The dish tastes best after being stored in the refrigerator overnight and reheated.

— Ingredients —

Black lentils, whole (*urad daal*) — *300 gms/1¼ cups*
Chilli powder — *5 gms/1 tsp*
Cream — *160 ml/²/₃ cup*
Garlic paste — *20 gms/4 tsp*
Ginger paste — *20 gms/4 tsp*

Salt to taste
Tomato purée — *160 ml/²/₃ cup*
White butter — *120 gms/½ cup*

— Steps —

1. Pick, clean and soak *daal* for at least 3 hours; best soaked overnight.

2. Add 1.5 litres water to the *daal* and cook over a low flame till grain splits and *daal* is mashed. It is traditionally cooked over charcoal embers for 6 hours or overnight with 2 litres/ 8½ cups of water. It can also be cooked for 12 hours in a slow cooker.

3. Stir the lentils vigorously to mash them.

4. Add the tomato purée, ginger and garlic pastes, salt and chilli powder and cook for an hour till *daal* is thick.

5. Keep aside 10 gms butter and add the rest to the *daal* along with the cream and cook for another 15 minutes, stirring continuously till the fat is incorporated into the *daal*.

TIPS

Time: Preparation: overnight
Cooking: 2½ hours on a gas stove;
overnight on charcoal or a slow cooker.

To serve: Add the reserved butter and
serve hot with any Indian bread.

PALAK PANEER

SERVES: 4

A classic north Indian recipe.

— Ingredients —

Spinach (*palak*) leaves — *1 kg*
Cottage cheese (*paneer*) cubes — *250 gms/1¼ cups*
Cream — *10 gms/2 tsp*
Ghee (clarified butter) — *30 gms/2 tbs*
Ginger, cut fine — *25 gms/5 tsp*
Green chillies, chopped — *3*
Maize flour (*makki ka atta*) — *20 gms/4 tsp*
Onions, chopped — *25 gms/5 tsp*
Red chilli powder — *5 gms/1 tsp*
Salt to taste
Tomatoes, finely cut — *10 gms/2 tsp*
Water — *2 litres/10 cups*

— Steps —

1. Remove the stalks of the spinach leaves. Wash very well and cut fine. Add water and salt and cook for 10 minutes. Drain the excess water and purée in a blender.

2. Add the *paneer* cubes to the purée and mix well. Add maize flour slowly and cook for 10 minutes. (This acts as a thickening agent.)

3. In a separate pan, heat the ghee. Brown the onions and most of the ginger. Add red chilli powder and stir. Pour this sauce over the paneer-spinach mixture. Stir well and cook through for 5 minutes.

TIPS

Time: Preparation: 25 minutes
Cooking: 30 minutes

To serve: Garnish with the remaining pieces of ginger, tomato pieces, green chillies and cream. Serve with a green salad and naan.

SHAHI PANEER

SERVES: 4

Cottage cheese curried in yoghurt with cashewnuts.

— Ingredients —

Cottage cheese (*paneer*), small cubes — *1 kg*
Bay leaves (*tej patta*) — *2*
Cardamom powder — *3 gms/²/₃ tsp*
Cashewnut paste — *10 gms/2 tsp*
Cinnamon sticks — *3*
Cloves — *6*
Coriander powder — *5 gms/1 tsp*
Double cream — *120 ml/²/₃ cup*
Garam masala — *8 gms/1²/₃ tsp*
Garlic paste — *40 gms/2²/₃ tbs*
Salt to taste
Ginger paste — *40 gms/2²/₃ tbs*
Green cardamoms — *6*
Mace powder (*javitri*) — *3 gms/²/₃ tsp*
Oil — *80 ml/5¹/₃ tbs*
Onions, quartered, boiled and ground — *200 gms/1 cup*
Red chilli powder — *10 gms/2 tsp*
Saffron (dissolved in 15 ml milk) — *0.5 gms*
Turmeric powder (*haldi*) — *4 gms/³/₄ tsp*
Vetivier (*kewda*) — *3 drops*
Yoghurt, made from cream, whisked — *180 gms/³/₄ cup*

— Steps —

1. Heat oil in a pan. Add cloves, bay leaves, cinnamon stick and green cardamoms. Sauté over medium heat until they begin to crackle. Add the onion paste and sauté for 2-3 minutes.

2. Add the ginger and garlic pastes, red chilli, turmeric powder, coriander powder, cashewnut paste and salt.

3. Add the paneer cubes, stir and cook for 5 minutes.

4. Add the whisked yoghurt and half a cup of warm water, bring it to a slow boil and then simmer until the oil separates from the gravy. Reduce heat.

5. Add the cream, cardamom powder, garam masala, mace powder, vetivier and saffron mixture.

TIPS

Time: Preparation: 30 minutes
Cooking: 20 minutes

To serve: Serve with any dry vegetable preparation and rotis.

KADHI

SERVES: 4

*A tangy yoghurt and gram flour based gravy
with gram flour dumplings floating in it.*

— Ingredients —

Yoghurt — *360 gms/1½ cups*	Oil to deep fry
Gram flour (*besan*)	Onion rounds (¼" thick)
— *120 gms/½ cup*	— *150 gms*
Carom (*ajwain*) seeds	Potatoes, cut round
— *2.5 gms/½ tsp*	— *150 gms*
Cumin (*jeera*) seeds	Red chilli powder
— *2.5 gms/½ tsp*	— *5 gms/1 tsp*
Fenugreek (*methi*) seeds	Red chillies, whole
— *1.25 gms/¼ tsp*	— *4*
Green chillies, chopped — *5*	Salt to taste
Groundnut oil — *60 ml/4 tbs*	Soda bi-carb — *a pinch*
Mustard (*sarson*) seeds —	Turmeric (*haldi*) powder
1.25 gms/¼ tsp	— *5 gms/1 tsp*

— Steps —

1. Whisk yoghurt, salt, red chilli powder,
turmeric and half the gram flour together in a
bowl. Keep aside.
2. Sieve the other half of the gram flour and
soda bi-carb together, add the carom seeds
and mix enough water to make a thick
batter. Beat well. Add green chillies.
3. Heat enough oil in a kadhai to deep fry.
Drop large spoonfuls of the batter in oil to get
1½" puffy dumplings. Fry till golden brown
on both sides. Remove and keep aside.
4. Heat 45 ml/3 tablespoons oil in a handi,
add the yoghurt mixture and 720 ml/3 cups
water. Bring to a boil, reduce to a low heat and
simmer for 8-10 minutes, stirring constantly to
avoid the yoghurt from curdling.
5. Add the potatoes and onions and cook till potatoes
are done.

7. Add the dumplings and simmer for 3 minutes.
8. Heat the remaining 15 ml/1 tablespoon oil in a small frying pan. Add the cumin, mustard and fenugreek seeds and saute till the cumin crackles. Add the whole red chillies. Stir.
9. Pour this tempering over the simmering hot kadhi.

TIPS

Time: Preparation: 45 minutes
Cooking: 30 minutes

To serve: Remove to a bowl and serve with boiled rice.

POTATO CREOLE

SERVES: 4

A spicy potato preparation.

— Ingredients —

Potatoes, boiled and cubed — *900 gms/4½ cups*	Oil — *80 ml/5⅓ tbs*
Butter — *20 gms/4 tsp*	Onions, chopped — *100 gms/½ cup*
Coriander powder — *8 gms/1⅔ tsp*	Red chilli powder — *10 gms/2 tsp*
Garlic, chopped — *20 gms/4 tsp*	Red chillies, whole, cut into half — *5*
Ginger, chopped — *20 gms/4 tsp*	Salt for seasoning
Green chillies, chopped — *10 gms/2 tsp*	Tomatoes, skinned and chopped — *300 gms/1½ cups*
Lemon juice — *15 ml/1 tbs*	Turmeric powder (*haldi*) — *5 gms/1 tsp*
Mustard seeds — *5 gms/1 tsp*	

— Steps —

1. Heat the oil in a pan. Sauté the whole red chillies and mustard seeds over medium heat until they begin to crackle.

2. Add the chopped onions, garlic, ginger and saute over high heat for 5-6 minutes. Add the red chilli powder, turmeric powder, coriander powder and salt and stir.

3. Add the chopped tomatoes and simmer on low heat until the oil separates from the gravy.

4. Add the boiled potato cubes, chopped green chillies, lemon juice and salt, stir and cook for 5 minutes.

TIPS

Time: Preparation: 10 minutes
Cooking: 30 minutes

To serve: Melt the butter and pour over the potatoes before serving. Garnish with green coriander.

Buttered Vegetables

SERVES: 4

Tastes wonderful when fresh vegetables are used.

— Ingredients —

Beans (green) — *200 gms*
Carrots — *2/200 gms*
Potatoes — *2-3/200 gms*
Cauliflower
— *2 cups/200 gms*
Green peas— *1 cup/100 gms*
Red pumpkin
— *1 cup/200 gms*
Butter — *250 gms*
Cream — *½ cup/150 ml*
Garlic paste — *3 tbs/40 gms*

Ginger paste — *3 tbs/40 gms*
Green chillies — *5*
Green coriander
— *½ cups/25 gms*
Kasoori methi (dry
fenugreek leaves) — *15 gms*
Red chilli powder
— *1 tbs/5 gms*
Salt to taste
Tomatoes — *10-12/1 kg*

— Steps —

1. Wash, peel and cut vegetables into 1 cm dices.
2. To make gravy, melt half the butter in a thick bottom pan. Add ginger and garlic paste. Stir and add tomatoes, salt, red chilli powder and approximately 500 ml of water, cover and simmer till tomatoes are mashed.
3. Cool and strain gravy through a fine sieve.
4. In a kadhai/wok, melt remaining butter, sauté green chillies over medium heat and add the cut vegetables. Stir for 4 minutes, pour the gravy and let it simmer till vegetables are cooked.
5. Add cream and fenugreek leaves. Adjust seasoning.

TIPS

Time: Preparation: 1 hour
Cooking: 45 minutes

To serve: Serve topped with a whirl of cream and chopped coriander.

GLOSSARY

Alu: Potato.

Amchoor: Dried mango powder. Lemon juice may be used as a substitute.

Aniseed (Sweet cumin): Aromatic seeds used in meat dishes.

Aromatic garam masala (Chana masala): Ingredients: Green cardamoms 175 gms; cumin seeds 120 gms; black pepper corns 120 gms; cinnamon (2.5 cms) 25 sticks; cloves 15 gms; nutmegs, 2. Makes 440 gms. Method: Grind all the ingredients to a fine powder. Sieve and store in an airtight container.

Asafoetida (Heeng): A pungent resin used in powdered form.

Baigan (Aubergine, Egg plant, Brinjal): Used whole, or in pieces.

Basmati rice: A fine long-grain rice grown mainly in India.

Bay leaf (Tej patta): An aromatic leaf used for flavouring.

Black beans (Urad dal): A black lentil, used whole or split.

Black lentils (Masoor dal): Also known as red split lentils.

Capsicum: Green bell pepper.

Cardamom, green (Chhoti elaichi): A plant of the ginger family whose seeds are used in flavouring.

Cardamom, large black (Badi elaichi): Used in many vegetable and meat dishes, its black pods are used ground whole.

Carom seeds (Ajwain): Also known as thymol or omum seeds.

Cauliflower (Gobi): Used whole or as flowerets to make a dry curry.

Chaat masala: Ingredients: Cumin seeds 65 gms; black pepper corns, black salt (pounded) and common salt 60 gms each; dry mint leaves 30 gms; carom seeds, asafoetida (pounded) 5 gms each; mango powder 150 gms; ginger powder, yellow chilli powder 20 gms each. Makes 445 gms. Method: Grind cumin seeds, pepper-corns, mint leaves and asafoetida together. Transfer to a bowl, mix remaining ingredients. Sieve and store in an airtight container.

Chillies, green (Hari mirch): Fresh chillies used for flavouring and tempering.

Chillies, whole dried red (Sabut mirch): More pungent than green chillies.

Chilli powder (Mirch pisi): Ground dried red chillies.

Cinnamon (Dalchini): An aromatic bark used as a spice.

Clarified butter (Ghee): Made at home but also available commercially.

Cloves (Lavang): Dried flower bud of a tropical plant, used as a spice.

Coconut, grated fresh: Method: Remove the coconut flesh from the hard shell with a knife and grate.

Coconut milk, fresh: Method: Put 2 cups of grated coconut into a food processor. Add 3 cups of water and blend. Sieve and squeeze out all the liquid. Use liquid. Excellent quality tinned coconut milk is available.

Coconut, creamed: Creamed coconut is easily available and can be converted into coconut milk by adding $^2/_3$ cup hot water to $^1/_3$ cup of creamed coconut.

Coriander, fresh green (Chinese parsley or Hara dhania): A herb used for seasoning and garnishing.

Coriander seeds, whole/ground (Dhania): Seeds of the coriander plant.

Cottage cheese (Paneer): Method: Boil 3 litres of milk. Add the juice of one lemon and stir till the mixture curdles. Remove from the fire. Cover and keep aside for 10 minutes. Strain the mixture through a piece of cheese cloth. Tie the ends of cloth together, squeeze out all the liquid, and place under a heavy weight for a few hours. The cheese (300 gms) is now ready for use.

Cumin seeds (Jeera): Available whole; may be powdered.

Cumin seeds, black (Shah jeera, Kala jeera): A caraway-like seed with a flavour that is more subtle than that of ordinary cumin; to be used sparingly.

Curry leaves, fresh and dried (Kari patta): Highly aromatic leaves. Use fresh.

Dals: Dried lentils. The word is used loosely for all pulses.

Dried milk (Khoya): A milk preparation made by evaporating creamy fresh milk. Use milk powder instead.

Dum cooking: This technique is used to improve the flavour of a dish by the method of sealing the lid, generally with dough and cooking on a low flame.

Fennel seeds (Saunf): These seeds are larger but look and taste like aniseeds.

Fenugreek leaves (Methi): A leafy vegetable, considered to be a great delicacy.

Fenugreek leaves, dried (Kasoori methi): Grown only in the Kasoor region of Pakistan, its dried leaves are used in chicken and lamb preparations.

Fenugreek seeds (Methe): Yellow, square and flat seeds with a bitter flavour.

Garam masala: Ingredients: Cumin seeds 90 gms; black peppercorns 70 gms; black cardamom seeds 75 gms; fennel seeds 30 gms; green cardamoms 40 gms; coriander seeds 30 gms; cloves, mace powder, black cumin seeds, 20 gms each; cinnamon (2.5 cms) 20 sticks; bay leaves 15 gms; ginger powder 15 gms; nutmegs 3. Makes 445 gms. Method: Grind all the ingredients except the ginger powder. Transfer to a clean bowl, add ginger powder and mix well. Sieve and store in an airtight container.

Ginger (Adrak): A root with a pungent flavour. Peel the skin before use.

Gram flour (Besan): A binding agent, used mainly as a batter.

Mace (Javitri): The outer membrane of nutmeg, used as a flavouring agent.

Maize flour (Makki ka atta): Flour made from Indian corn.

Melon seeds (Magaz): Peeled melon seeds are used in savoury dishes.

Mint leaves (Pudina): A herb, used fresh or dried.

Mustard oil (Sarson ka tel): An edible oil extracted from mustard seeds.

Mustard seeds, black (Sarson): A pungent seed, widely used in Indian food.

Nigella Indica (Kalonji): Used in Indian breads, vegetables and fish.

Nutmeg (Jaiphal): A spice, used grated or ground for flavouring sweets and curies.

Parsley: Can be a substitute for green coriander leaves.

Pistachios (Pista): A dried fruit, used in sweetmeats and biryanis.

Pomegranate seeds (Anardana): Used in savouries, and to give a sour flavour.

Poppy seeds (Khus khus): Tiny white seeds used for flavouring.

Rose water (Gulab jal): A flavouring made of fresh rose petals.

Saffron (Kesar/Zafran): The stigma of the crocus flower, grown in the Kashmir valley. Known as the king of spices, it is used for its rich yellow colouring and flavour. Dissolve in water or warm milk before use.

Sambar powder: Ingredients: Coriander seeds 150 gms; cumin seeds 100 gms; black pepper corns 40 gms; mustard seeds 40 gms; fenugreek seeds 40 gms; red chilli, whole 40 gms; turmeric powder 25 gms; Bengal gram 80 gms; urad dal 80 gms; oil 50 ml; garlic powder 20 gms; ginger powder 20 gms; Makes 600 gms. Method: Heat the oil. Sauté all the ingredients on very low heat until evenly coloured. Cool and grind to a fine powder.

Sesame seeds (Til): An oil-yielding seed used for sweets and savouries.

Split green beans (Moong ki dal): A type of lentil, used split or whole.

Spinach (Palak): A leafy green vegetable.

Tamarind (Imli): A pod-like, sour fruit, used as a souring agent.

Turmeric (Haldi): A root of the ginger family used for colouring, flavouring and for its antiseptic qualities.

Toovar dal (Pigeon peas): Also known as toor or arhar dal.

Vetivier (Kewda): An extract made from the flowers of the kewda (*pandanus*) plant used extensively as a flavouring.

Yoghurt (Dahi): Made from milk and used extensively in curries and biryani. Drained yoghurt can be obtained by drip-drying the yoghurt in a fine muslin or cheesecloth for 4 to 6 hours.